Visions of San Miguel
The Heartland of Mexico

COVER: Flamenco dancer performing in front of *La Parroquia*. PHOTO: RAUL TOUZON
INSIDE COVER: 1740 lace pattern adapted from Atotonilco sanctuary. PHOTO: RAUL TOUZON DIGITAL COLLAGE: CHUCK JONES
LEFT: Acrobat performing in front of *La Parroquia*. PHOTO: AMANDA MOULSON

INTRODUCTION

What is it about San Miguel that attracts so many artists and sparks such creative expression? Is it the extraordinary light? The awe-inspiring colonial architecture? The soothing climate? The colorful and complex culture? The historical significance? What magical mixture continues to make San Miguel such a cauldron of creativity?

Through the eyes of 30 talented photographers, *Visions of San Miguel, the Heartland of Mexico*, explores this creative energy. Each image conveys a unique glimpse into the life and soul of this charming hillside community.

In celebrating the spirit of San Miguel, this vibrant collection of photographs endeavors to enlighten, entertain and inform. Above all, it seeks to express appreciation for the people on both sides of the lens.

Gratitude to the talented photographers whose generous gifts of artistry shapes *Visions of San Miguel, The Heartland of Mexico.*

Enrich your imagination with the joyous spirit of San Miguel as captured on these pages.

Statue of St. Michael in front of
La Parroquia. PHOTO: *Atención*

Panoramic view of San Miguel, circa 1930. PHOTO: ARTURO SUAREZ

DEDICATION

In memory of Galen and Barbara Cushman Rowell, whose lives touched and inspired us all. DK

To my pal, "Muffet," whose wonderful spirit mirrored the magic and charm of San Miguel de Allende. ASD

TABLE OF CONTENTS

PHOTO: FRED EDISON

FOUNDATIONS OF GREATNESS

The town of San Miguel de Allende is called *La Fragua de Independencia*, the place where the movement to gain national independence from Spain was forged and created. It was here that revolutionaries from all parts of the land met to formulate, strategize and coordinate their united fight against Spanish rule.

The struggle included members of all economic and cultural levels; from *criollos* (people born here with Spanish parents), *mestizos* (people of mixed Spanish and Indian blood) and the *indios* and *mulattos* (darker skinned indigenous people) as well as members of the clergy.

Native son and *criollo*, Ignacio Allende, enlisted the support of Father Hidalgo from nearby Dolores and together with Aldama and Jiménez, other heroes of the Revolution, led the movement to start the fight against Spain. Although this first effort was to prove unsuccessful, finally, on November 10, 1824, the United States of Mexico was created and all of its inhabitants became united as one. *¡Viva México!*

PHOTO: BILL BEGALKE

San Francisco Street with the *Presidencia* on the left and *el Jardin* on the right. HISTORICAL PHOTO

Looking up Canal Street with *La Parroquia* on the right and the dome of *Las Monjas* on the left. HISTORICAL PHOTO

El Jardin, showing *Portales de Guadalupe* and the clock tower circa 1870. HISTORICAL PHOTO

The public laundry, in its original location in front of *El Chorro*.
PHOTO: Arturo Suarez

Plaza de la Soledad (now *Plaza Civica*) showing the Church of Our Lady of Health, *La Salud* (right) and the *Oratorio de San Felipe Neri* (left) and the public market held in front, circa 1870.

HISTORICAL PHOTO

San Antonio church before completion of the bell tower.
PHOTO: ARTURO SUAREZ

COBBLESTONES OF COLOR

Rich, textural color is visible everywhere in San Miguel. Around every corner and within every doorway, a visual surprise awaits to delight the eye.

In this chapter, images of people, architecture, markets, artisans, historic buildings and street scenes are captured by a diverse group of talented photographers, each with a unique perspective.

PHOTO: GLENDA KAPSALIS

Casa Luna dining room. PHOTO: DOUGLAS STEAKLEY

Casa Luna patio. PHOTO: LOUIS CANTILLO

View of *Las Monjas* dome. PHOTO: LOUIS CANTILLO

The famous carved Canal doors adorn one of the most impressive houses in San Miguel. Located on the *Jardin*, the neo-classical residence was built in the late 18th century. PHOTO: RAUL TOUZON

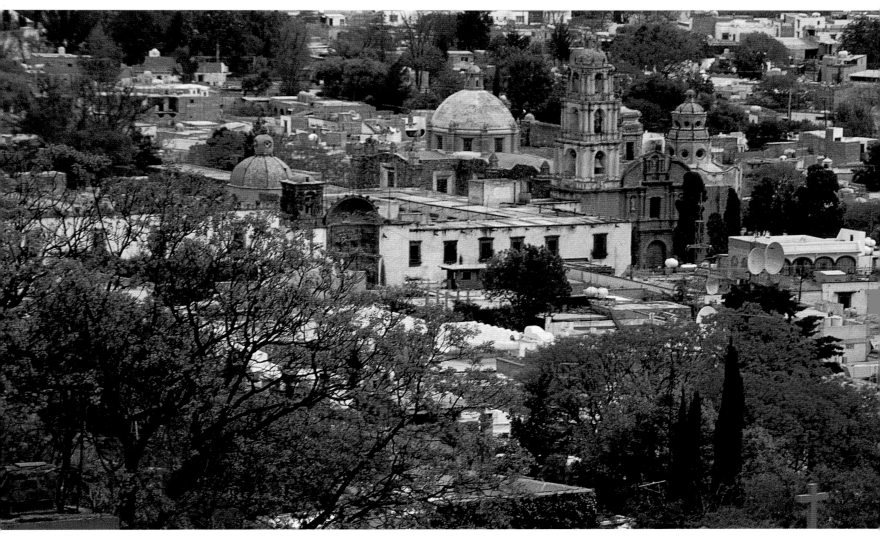

Brilliant purple jacaranda trees dot San Miguel's landscape in the spring. The domes and towers in the background are of churches located on the *Plaza Civica*. PHOTO: DIXON ADAMS

PHOTO: CHUCK JONES

PHOTO: FRED EDISON

PLAZA CIVICA, LOCATED NORTH-EAST OF THE JARDIN, boasts the greatest concentration of religious architecture in San Miguel. Dominating the plaza is the Church of our Lady of Health, *La Salud*, topped by a stone-carved shell, symbolic of conch shells carried by early missionaries who used them to baptize the native Indian inhabitants. A large statue of General Ignacio Allende, local hero and leader in the fight for independence from Spain, commands the center of the plaza.

Painting *plein air* on Aldama Street. PHOTO: *Atención*

THE ARTS AND ARTISTS flourish in San Miguel, well-known for its creative climate.

The artist's subject, Aldama Street.
PHOTO: AMANDA MOULSON

Mural painted by Pedro Martinez in 1940, in the style made famous by Diego Rivera.
PHOTO: CHUCK JONES

THE BELLAS ARTES IS A BRANCH OF the Mexican government's national system for promotion of art and culture. It is housed in what used to be the cloister of the former convent of the Church of *La Concepcion*, locally known as *Las Monjas* (the nuns). Built in the mid-1700s, the beautiful courtyard is surrounded by galleries, rooms for classes in the arts, an auditorium and a cafe.

Mural by celebrated artist David Alfaro Siquieros. The subject of this dramatic painting depicts the life of Ignacio Allende. The project begun, in 1946, by Siquieros and his students was never completed. PHOTO: CHUCK JONES

The magnificent dome of *Las Monjas* can be seen from the *Bellas Artes* courtyard. The dome was modeled after *Les Invalides* in Paris by the same builder, Zeferino Gutierrez, who copied the facade of the *Parroquia* from postcards of gothic-European cathedrals. PHOTO: CHUCK JONES

San Miguel abstract street scene.
PHOTO: ELSMARIE NORBY

More textured walls. PHOTO: DON WOLF

First Communion excitement.
PHOTO: WILLIAM D. THOMPSON

Quincañera, a girl of 15, dressed up for her coming-of-age party.
PHOTO: SONDRA ZELL

Portrait of a woman with tiled wall. PHOTO: JILL GENSER

30

PHOTO: ALYCE PAGANO

PHOTO: JILL GENSER

PHOTO: ED FOLEY

Gitano, a beautiful Clydesdale horse, marches into town on weekends towing a turn-of-the-century ice cream cart—to the delight of children and adults alike. PHOTO: RAUL TOUZON

Luz Maria, the rose vendor.
PHOTO: ELSMARIE NORBY

Portales Allende, on the west side of the *Jardin*. PHOTO: NED BROWN

Children bathing in tubs at the public laundry. PHOTO: DON WOLF

Women washing clothes at the public laundry near Juarez Park. PHOTO: *Atención*

Two women catching up. PHOTO: ALYCE PAGANO

Broom vendor. PHOTO: DON WOLF

Elder with basket. PHOTO: DON WOLF

Plastics vendor. PHOTO: DON WOLF

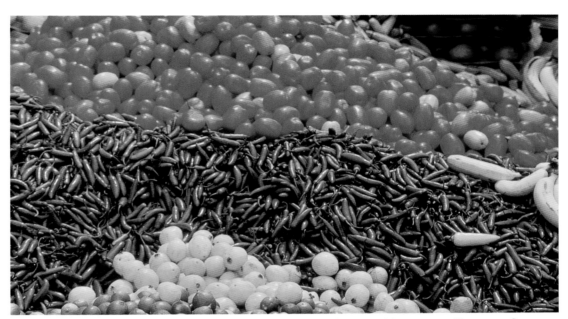

A riot of colorful vegetables. PHOTO: DOUGLAS STEAKLY

Fruit and fruit drinks. PHOTO: ED FOLEY

Cactus preparation. PHOTO: DOUGLAS STEAKLEY

Who wants a chicken? PHOTO: ED FOLEY

Flower vendors catch up on the news. PHOTO: NED BROWN

Dr. Leopoldo Estrada, creates *mojigangas*, (giant *papel maché* figures)
that people wear to parade in during *fiestas*. PHOTO: JENNIFER HAAS

An experienced potter. PHOTO: CHUCK JONES

Don Eduardo, woodcarver and folk artist. PHOTO: JENNIFER HAAS

Fabio, on the roof deck of *Casa Luna*, with a view of *Las Monjas* dome. PHOTO: J BYRON SMITH

Street dog wannabes. PHOTO: CHUCK JONES

San Miguel street dogs. PHOTO: JILL GENSER

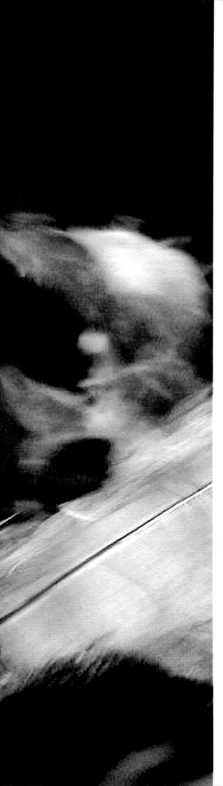

Fiestas, Fiestas and More Fiestas

Even before Mexico's independence from Spain in 1826, the village of San Miguel was famous for its *fiestas*. Rumor has it that in the 1700s a Spanish Viceroy ordered the populace to stop celebrating and to get back to work.

It seems apparent the people of San Miguel were not influenced by the Viceroy's dictum and refused to comply—and so we have *Fiestas, Fiestas and More Fiestas* today and most every day, here in the town that loves to celebrate.

The pages in this section capture only a small portion of the hundreds of celebrations that take place in festive San Miguel.

PHOTO: WILLIAM D. THOMPSON

A man representing local hero, Ignacio Allende, rides into town. PHOTO: DAVE FOGG

Flags and fireworks. PHOTO: SUE BEERE

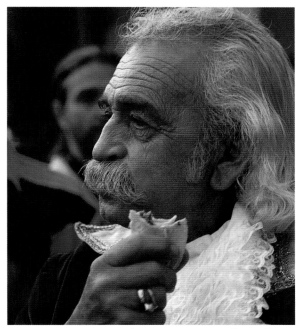

Aristocrat. PHOTO: DAVE FOGG

Country person. PHOTO: DAVE FOGG

FIESTAS PATRIAS

From September 15 until the beginning of October can be compared to a continuous 4th of July or Bastille Day celebration here in Mexico. Patriotism runs high, while celebrating Mexico's fight for independence from Spain.

EVERY YEAR ON SEPTEMBER 15, at 11 pm, _El Grito_, the reenactment of Father Hidalgo's momentous speech to begin the revolt against Spain, takes place throughout Mexico. In San Miguel, this patriotic event is lavishly celebrated with pageantry, music and fireworks. Throngs of patriots cheer when a marathon runner arrives with a torch, symbolizing the delivery in 1810 of a crucial message from a co-conspirator in Queretaro to Ignacio Allende in San Miguel.

Ignacio Perez, Mexico's Paul Revere, carried the message from the wife of the governor of Queretaro, Josefa Ortiz de Dominque, to Ignacio Allende.

Allende then forwarded the message to Father Hidalgo in Dolores, who proceeded to ring the church bells signalling the beginning of the revolution. Then Father Hidalgo delivered that famous, stirring _Grito_, a cry for independence from Spain. _¡Viva México!_

PHOTO: _Atención_

51

Running through the sparks. PHOTO: ED FOLEY

CASTILLOS ARE TALL bamboo-like frames built to support colorful, shooting fireworks which fly off into the night sky—and sometimes into the crowds watching the show.

Boy protected by a box races below a *castillo*. PHOTO: FRED EDISON

PHOTO: FRED EDISON

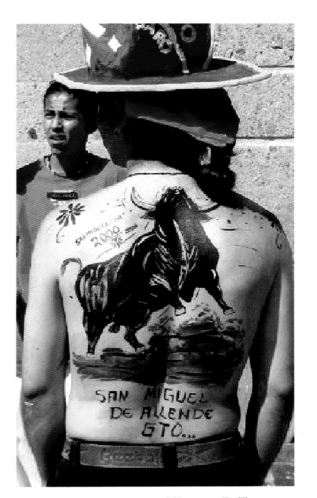

ADRENALINE, BEER AND BLOOD RUN HIGH during the *San Miguelada*, also called the *Pamplonada*, after the running of the bulls in Spain. Held the weekend between *El Grito,* September 15 and the celebration of *St. Michael's Fiesta*, September 29, the town is packed with young people from all over Mexico—who celebrate in exuberant style.

PHOTO: RAUL TOUZON

PICADORES PLAY AN IMPORTANT ROLE in traditional bullfights. From atop heavily protected horses they lance the bull's neck, cutting ligaments, which causes the animal to lower his head. Thus the *matador* is able to fight the disabled bull on foot using cape and sword.

PHOTO: RAUL TOUZON

Bullfighting. PHOTO: NED BROWN

Traditional *matador*.
PHOTO: NED BROWN

Rejoneador, Portuguese-style bullfighter, in action. PHOTO: FRED EDISON

Charra. PHOTO: JILL GENSER

CHARROS (MALES) AND CHARRAS (FEMALES) entertain crowds with their
skilled horsemanship and distinctive costumes.

Charro riding into town. PHOTO: CARL SCOFIELD

XUCHILES ARE OFFERINGS OF FLOWERS built upon platforms constructed of reeds and sticks. The structure is covered with matting made from the interior of a cactus called *cucharilla* meaning little spoon, based upon their spoon-like shape. Interspersed among this webbing, colorful flowers are placed to form crosses and other symbols. Each *xuchile* platform is escorted to decorate the *Parroquia* by the people who created them.

PHOTO: DIXON ADAMS

63

PHOTO: WILLIAM D. THOMPSON

PHOTO: WILLIAM D. THOMPSON

PHOTO: GLENDA KAPSALIS

DURING THE SEPTEMBER FIESTAS, *Volodores de Papantla* (flying dancers from Papantla, on the Gulf Coast) come to San Miguel to entertain the crowds. In symbolic costume, the five men climb a 60' pole that's erected in front of the *Parroquia*. Their pre-Hispanic ritual is a supplication to the gods of the sun, wind, earth and water, that their lives and those of others will be fruitful and productive.

PHOTO: WILLIAM D. THOMPSON

Matachines representing the Spanish Moors. PHOTO: ED FOLEY

PHOTO: ED FOLEY

THE CONFLICT BETWEEN THE SPANIARDS and the indigenous
people is enacted with colorful costumes during the September *fiestas*.

68

PHOTO: William D. Thompson

PHOTO: Richard Krieger

PHOTO: DON WOLF

ST. MICHAEL'S FIESTA

According to the Bible, St. Michael the Archangel defeated Lucifer, the devil, thus symbolizing the triumph of good over evil and life over death. How fitting that St. Michael is the patron saint of this town where the fight for freedom from Spain was forged. During the *Fiesta of St. Michael*, the weekend of, or after, September 29, parades, music, dancing and pageantry abound with statues, devils, Indians in death masks, and, of course, fireworks.

PHOTO: GLENDA KAPSALIS

PHOTO: WILLIAM D. THOMPSON

DURING THE FIESTA OF ST. MICHAEL, dancers from all over Mexico perform around the *Jardin* in their distinctive regional costumes, proudly showing off their local traditions.

Ofrenda to a musician. PHOTO: *Atención*

THE DAY OF THE DEAD

Día de los Muertos is celebrated for children on November 1 and for adults on November 2. *Ofrendas*, or altars, are created to honor the spirits of the departed.

Sugar skulls and figures to place
on *ofrendas*. PHOTO: *Atención*

Honoring the Twin Towers. PHOTO: SONDRA ZELL

Children and *ofrenda*. PHOTO: CARL SCOFIELD

Remembering the departed at the cemetary,
lighting candles and decorating gravesites.
PHOTO: GALEN ROWELL/MOUNTAIN LIGHT

Day of the Dead altar.
PHOTO: ED FOLEY

PHOTO: GALEN ROWELL,
MOUNTAIN LIGHT

PHOTO: JOYCE AARON

A girl dressed as *Adelita* symbolizes the women involved in the Revolution. PHOTO: RAUL TOUZON.

Revolutionary. PHOTO: RAUL TOUZON

REVOLUTION DAY

Porfirio Díaz became the President of Mexico in 1877. He ruled the country as a dictator for 33 years until ousted after several years of a bloody, national struggle. Revolutionaries, including Pancho Villa, Zapata, Madero, Carranza and Obregón fought against each other as well as against the Díaz regime. Finally, on November 20, 1911 Díaz fled to France. In 1917 the Constitution of Mexico was adopted. Every November 20th, children dressed as Revolutionaries parade with patriotic pride and dignity throughout town.

Cristeros, country Revolutionaries. PHOTO: FRED EDISON

Aristocratas, wealthy Revolutionaries. PHOTO: RAUL TOUZON

RICH AND POOR JOINED TOGETHER in the Revolution of 1910, which resulted in the adoption of the Mexican Constitution, in 1917.

82

PHOTO: DIXON ADAMS

CHRISTMAS IS A joyful time in San Miguel. The festivities begin on December 16 and continue to Three King's Day, January 6.

Every night from December 16 through Christmas Eve, *Posadas* take place. Children dressed up as Mary and Joseph parade through town knocking on doors asking for lodging. Finally they arrive at an inn, or *posada*, where they are permitted to stay in the manger, represented by Christmas crèche scenes.

At contemporary *Posadas*, the designated neighborhood home welcomes Mary, Joseph and their procession to come inside and break open *piñatas* filled with candy. Then everyone celebrates by eating traditional Christmas food of *tomales* and *ponche*.

PHOTO: WILLIAM D. THOMPSON

PHOTO: ED FOLEY

EVERY MAY 21, CHILDREN ARE costumed as flowers, bugs and birds to welcome spring. *La Reina,* or queen, adorned with crown and sash, is selected to grace a float.

ALL PHOTOS: ED FOLEY

El Señor de la Columna. PHOTO: DOUGLAS STEAKLEY

Arrival of first Easter procession from Atotonilco.

EASTER CELEBRATIONS

Two Sundays before Easter a procession of thousands arrives into San Miguel at dawn after an all-night pilgrimage from the Sanctuary of Atotonilco about 10 miles from town. Accompanied by thundering fireworks and ringing church

PHOTO: WILLIAM D. THOMPSON

Virgin of Dolores. PHOTO: WILLIAM D. THOMPSON

bells, pilgrims carry platforms bearing statues of saints. They walk upon chamomile-carpeted streets adorned with purple and white flags, balloons and other decorations amid throngs of spectators.

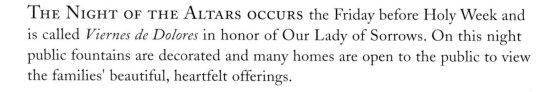

THE NIGHT OF THE ALTARS OCCURS the Friday before Holy Week and is called *Viernes de Dolores* in honor of Our Lady of Sorrows. On this night public fountains are decorated and many homes are open to the public to view the families' beautiful, heartfelt offerings.

HOME ALTAR PHOTOS: JO BRENZO

Ecce Homo. PHOTO: WILLIAM D. THOMPSON

PHOTOS: JO BRENZO

EASTER ALTARS ARE FILLED WITH ELEMENTS of symbolic significance. Bitter oranges represent the pain of the Virgin; palms signify her strength; gold-colored flags waving atop pierced oranges represent the connection between God and men; wheat grass symbolizes the Eucharist and the Palestinian roads Christ walked upon; colored water is a reminder of the Virgin's tears; chamomile, fennel and candy made from squash allude to the sweetness of the Virgin.

PHOTO: CARL SCOFIELD

PROCESSIONS OCCUR DAILY DURING Holy Week, which begins with Palm Sunday and ends with Easter Sunday.

CHILDREN FREQUENTLY DRESS AS angels and carry statues of saints.
Devout families reverently display cherished *Santos* in their homes.

NUMEROUS PROCESSIONS, decorated fountains and home altars dramatize the passion and spirituality of Holy Week.

PHOTO: JO BRENZO

PHOTO: PAUL FARDIG

DURING HOLY WEEK, the devout reenact the last days of Christ's
life, wearing crowns of thorns and bearing crosses.

PHOTO: SUE BEERE

98

PHOTO: JO BRENZO

ALL ASPECTS OF THE LAST WEEK of Christ's life are re-lived during
Holy Week, including Christ's trial and carrying the crucifixion cross.

PHOTO: JO BRENZO

PHOTO: FRED EDISON

EASTER SUNDAY IS THE CLIMAX OF HOLY WEEK, ending with a bang
and the blowing up of Judas figures in the *Jardin*. Today these *papel maché*
mannequins–filled with explosives–often resemble politicians, local businessmen,
and other irksome characters.

photo: Douglas Steakley

To celebrate St. Anthony, paraders, in outlandish costumes, dance through the streets tossing candy into the crowds.

LOCOS DAY, JUNE 12

ALL PHOTOS: JO BRENZO

PHOTO: WILLIAM D. THOMPSON

MUSIC AND MUSICIANS PLAY AN integral role in Mexican culture, and especially here in San Miguel. From *mariachis* in traditional garb to *indio* musicians in feathers to colorfully costumed flute and drum players, all celebrate and add to the festive atmosphere that makes San Miguel such a lively place to live and to visit.

PHOTO: William D. Thompson

PHOTO: *Atención*

PHOTO: RAUL TOUZON

SINCE SAN MIGUEL IS SUCH A romantic town, it attracts lovers
who want to solidify their union in marriage—often accompanied by
musicians, horse-drawn carriages, fireworks and more.

PHOTO: RAUL TOUZON

ALL VARIETIES OF WEDDINGS TAKE place in San Miguel—and all with blessings galore. Either on motorcycle or in the more traditional horse-drawn carriage, bride and groom glow in the love of their union.

PHOTO: FRED EDISON

Blessing of the taxis. PHOTO: PETER OLWYLER

SPIRITUALITY INFUSES ALL ASPECTS of life here in San Miguel. From the religious icons in niches on buildings and in cars, trucks and buses; to the sounds of bells reminding people to come to church; to the smell of *copal* wafting onto the streets; and the religious figures prominent in every marketplace, home and church. The next few pages depict some of these spiritual events.

113

Blessing of the
cowboys and horses.
PHOTO: RICHARD KRIEGER

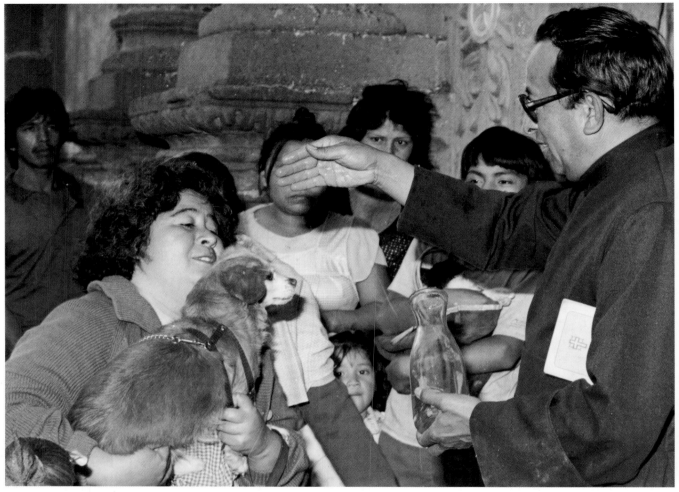

PHOTO: *Atención*

THE BLESSING OF THE ANIMALS OCCURS on St. Anthony's Day, January 17. Townspeople bring household pets as well as livestock to various churches to be blessed with holy water. On January 24, pilgrims depart for San Juan de los Lagos, about 145 miles from San Miguel.

PHOTO: PETER OLWYLER

114

La Parroquia:
Icon of the Heartland

La Parroquia, the Parish Church, also called the Church of St. Michael the Archangel, patron saint of San Miguel, dominates the landscape of town with its fantasy-like Gothic facade flanked by two bell towers. Its strategic location on the south side of the *Jardin* makes its presence part of the everyday life of residents and visitors.

Like a woman repeatedly changing her wardrobe, the *Parroquia* alters her appearance depending on the time of day, season, climate and mood. And, like any cherished object of affection, the *Parroquia* appears in a different light depending on which pair of eyes is looking at her and when.

The pages of this section portray the *Parroquia* through the viewfinders of several photographers, each with a different perspective—and each with a glorious expression of awe and appreciation.

La Parroquia with statue of *Fray Juan de San Miguel*,
founder of the town, in the foreground.
PHOTO: GALEN ROWELL/MOUNTAIN LIGHT

Parroquia with original facade. HISTORICAL PHOTO

THE PARROQUIA WE SEE TODAY WAS originally a smaller, more conventional church constructed from 1689 to 1730. In 1880, the primary two-story towers were demolished and master craftsman, Seferino Gutierrez, an unschooled full-blooded Indian, began the design and construction of the new façade. According to records, Gutierrez modeled his plan for the *Parroquia* from postcards of gothic European cathedrals. It is believed that the drawing, to the right, is a copy of his original design. It is said that Gutierrez would show his workers what to do each day by drawing their instructions in the sand.

Drawing for new facade. HISTORICAL PHOTO

Parroquia, circa 1930. PHOTO: ARTURO SUAREZ

120

PHOTO: LANCE TERRY

122

PHOTO: Amanda Moulson

PHOTO: RAUL TOUZON

PHOTO: ED FOLEY

PHOTO: DIXON ADAMS

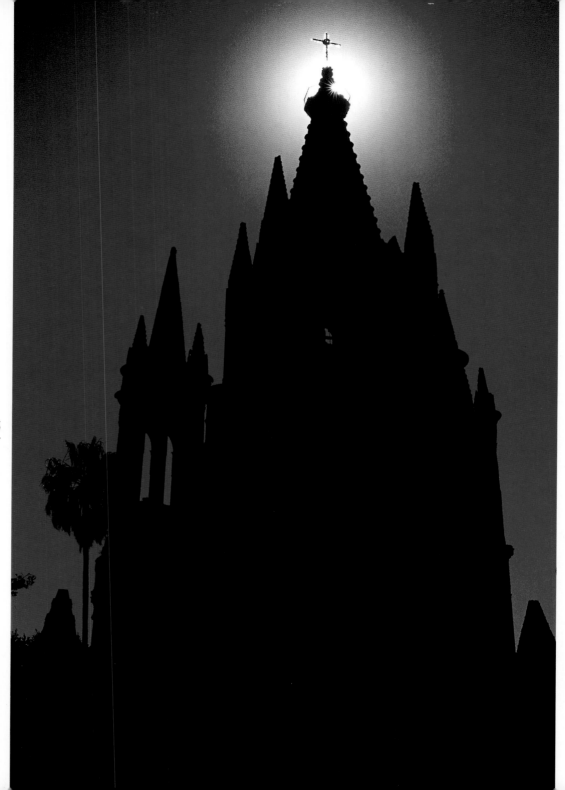

PHOTO: CHUCK JONES

ACKNOWLEDGEMENTS

Heartfelt thanks to the many photographers and artists who generously offered their images, support and encouragement for this book. We regret that we could include just a handful of the hundreds of photos submitted.

Kudos to Pat Tripp, book designer extraordinaire, whose artistic eye and computer skills made our *Visions of San Miguel, The Heartland of Mexico* come to life—not to mention her patience, dedication, humor and terrific organizational skills.

Special appreciation to Raul Touzon for his striking photographs, artistic photo-editing talents and helpful connections that opened so many doors for us.

To Chuck Jones, enormous gratitude not only for his artistic images, but also for his generous computer and photographic reproduction magic, which increased the quality of our book to the megamagnitude!

Gracias to William D. (Memo) Thompson for the generous use of his extensive inventory of photos, his computer wizardry and for introducing us to Eric Suarez, whose father's historic images grace these pages.

Mil gracias to Jill Genser for her lovely, personal photographs, as well as support and advice in editing. Thanks to the *Bellas Artes* and to *Atención* for access to their extensive archives.

To Susana Zermeno, thanks for taking care of business and being the best support person ever. To friend and colleague, Leandro Delgado, *muchas gracias* for the history lessons!

Compliments to Matthew Yim of Marwin Productions for his professional and friendly assistance shepherding our book through printing and production in Hong Kong.

And, last but not least, eternal gratitude to the warm people of San Miguel, whose spirit and soul make this town such an extraordinary place to live and to visit. ¡*Viva México!*

PHOTO: DIXON ADAMS

PHOTOGRAPHERS...

JOYCE AARON lives in New York and has been working in the theater for many years as an actor and director. She loves San Miguel and looks forward to spending more time here.

For 25 years, DIXON ADAMS has shot news, sports, advertising and stock photography. His photos have been featured in newspapers, magazines, tourist guides, web pages, calendars, directories and industrial publications. Recently, his focus has been providing pro bono photography for charitable organizations. Dixon and his wife, Bett, split their time between homes in San Miguel and Pensacola, FL. Reach Dixon at: **dixon@unisono.net.mx**

Born in New York, SUE BEERE moved to San Miguel in 1971. Her photos frequently appear in the local newspaper, *Atención*. For many years Sue assisted Peter Olwyler in his intensive photography workshops. Her specialty is photographing people and theatrical productions. Sue can be reached at: **olwyler@unisono.net.mx**

Author, photographer and San Miguel resident, BILL BEGALKE combines his love of travel, writing and photography into a successful freelance career that combines all three talents. An award-winning writer and TV documentarian, his work has appeared internationally in newspapers, magazines and web pages. See Bill's columns and photos on **www.mexconnect.com** or email him at: **casaoz@unisono.net.mx**

JO BRENZO, director of the *Academia de Fotografía* art school in San Miguel, is on the faculty of *Bellas Artes*. She has taught photography since 1979 and has conducted numerous workshops in the US and México. Jo's work has been exhibited throughout the world. She encourages and supports other artists and photographers through her *Galería de Fotográfico* located on Reloj #46 here in San Miguel. To see more of Jo's work, a schedule of events at her gallery and upcoming workshops, log on to: **www.acdphoto.com**

NED BROWN was born and raised in Brooklyn, NY but lived the majority of his life in California where he founded and operated a printing business. Ned started as an amateur photographer 20 years ago and studied with leading photographers in California and San Miguel. In 2001, Ned and his wife, Sally, purchased a home in San Miguel and now live here permanently. Ned can be reached at: **nedb_3@hotmail.com**

LOUIS CANTILLO was born in Caracas, Venezuela, and studied photography in Texas before moving to Arizona in 1992. Louis is best known for his vibrant landscape photography and an extensive collection of door and window images taken around the world. His work has been published internationally and shown in several galleries. To see more examples of his colorful photographs go to: **www.louiscantillo.com**

For 30 years, internationally acclaimed NBC photojournalist, FRED EDISON has captured images of dramatic, history-making events around the world. His work has been published in many books and magazines and he has received numerous honors and prestigious awards. Fred often said of his work, "I loved it so much I would have done it for free." Fred resides in San Miguel with his cameras, six standard poodles and wife, Janice. For more information, contact Fred at: **fredricobrovo@aol.com**

PAUL S. FARDIG is a professional engineer with the U.S. Public Health Service and a part-time photography instructor with the Montgomery County, (MD) Department of Recreation.

DAVE FOGG, a FOA (Friend of Archie), has been taking photographs since fifth grade. Dave's first visit to San Miguel was in 1998 when Archie arranged a high school reunion for 20 friends to experience the September *fiestas* here. He is a graduate of Yale University, and lives in Wakefield, RI where he works as a business writer, keynote speaker and executive coach. You can reach Dave at:
davis.fogg@verizon.net

Photographer **ED FOLEY,** has been a part-time resident of San Miguel for over 15 years. His highly detailed and fiercely colored images of Mexico have appeared in books, magazines and galleries. When he's not in Mexico, Ed resides in East Greenwich, RI with his dog, Bradley. He can be contacted at:
ohmygodwhatashot@aol.com

Tucson-based writer/photographer **JILL GENSER,** has been visiting San Miguel since 1995. Her gentle and spontaneous images are a wonderful reflection of her love for the region and its people. Jill is currently working on a project that celebrates the children of Mexico in both pictures and prose. She can be reached at either PO Box 65718, Tucson, AZ 85728 or at:
jgphoto222@earthlink.net

Originally from Spartanburg, SC, **JENNIFER HAAS** moved to San Miguel in 1966. She studied photography at the *Instituto Allende* under George Konduras. Her work has appeared in various exhibits throughout Mexico. Jennifer recently opened a small museum devoted to Latin American popular art near Atotonilco, about 20 minutes from San Miguel. The museum is open by appointment and Jennifer can be reached by phone. In San Miguel, call: **152-0804**

CHUCK JONES, born in May 1950 in Clarksburg, WV, has been a photographer since he was 11. Starting with his first Brownie, Chuck has shot and printed black and white, color and cibachrome over his 42-year career. He is a digital pioneer, who has worked extensively with most of the modern digital technologies in his "Digital Lightroom." His current passion in life is "painting pictures with his Leica." His work can be seen at *Galería Tecolote* in San Miguel, at "The Gallery" inside Meson del Tecolote in Pozos and at his Santa Fe, NM studio. Contact Chuck at:
chuckpjones@earthlink.net

GLENDA HAWLEY KAPSALIS is a fine art, documentary and commercial photographer, who shoots both black and white and color. Based in Evanston, IL, she also spends part of each year in Mexico and Greece. Glenda's exploration of people's loss of connection to the land brought on by urbanization and agribusiness takes her to remote villages and rural areas of Greece, Mexico and the heartland of the United States. To learn more about Glenda's art and to see more of her images log on to:
www.glendakapsalis.com

A retired high school principal from Homer, AK, **RICHARD KRIEGER** is an amateur photographer who combines his passion for travel with his love for photography. San Miguel is one of his favorite travel destinations. Currently, Richard is involved in environmental education in Alaska. Contact him at:
kriegers@xyz.net

AMANDA MOULSON a photographer and public relations executive, lives in Atlanta, GA. Amanda has travelled extensively in Central America, Europe and Africa and takes her camera every place she goes. Amanda specializes in documentary photography, particularly city life and street scenes. This is the first time her work has been published in a book. For more information about Amanda's work, visit:
www.amandamoulson.com

...AND MORE PHOTOGRAPHERS

ELSMARIE NORBY, of Scandinavian descent, now a San Miguel resident, has been taking photographs since her childhood. She has a passion for the documentation of life unfolding through images of people, events and the beauty of nature. To that end, her project "Flesh & Stones" is a portfolio of high-quality notecards—portraits of people taken right here on the streets of San Miguel. A portion of each sale is given to the person whose image it is that graces the card. Elsmarie can be reached at: **elsmarie@unisono.net.mx**

PETER OLWYLER moved to San Miguel in 1955 and until his death in 1999 he captured, through black and white photography, the special humanity of Mexican life—one he described as "the sense of self ... a stoicism, and above all, a feeling of personal dignity." At various times Peter was director of public relations as well as instructor of both photography and writing at the *Instituto Allende*. Along with his partner, Sue Beere, he worked on the English language newspaper, *Atención*. Over the years, he served as managing editor, writer and photographer. For more information about Peter and his work, please email: **olwyler@unisono.net.mx**

ALYCE GOMEZ PAGANO is a native of California, currently living in San Francisco. It was in 1988, that she and her husband, Jim, joined a camera club and her love of photography soared. Alyce began to win awards, had some of her images published in magazines and other media and has shown in various gallery exhibits. Alyce can be reached at: **alyce.pagano@wspan.com**

Internationally known photographer **GALEN ROWELL** received numerous accolades, including the Ansel Adams Award for his contribution to the art of wilderness photography. Galen's love of mountain climbing in combination with his artistic eye and 35mm camera sets the environment for the creation of what he calls "dynamic landscape— the unexpected convergence of light and form and seemingly unrepeatable moments captured by combining imagination and action with a clear understanding of outdoor optical phenomena." Galen's images have been reproduced in 17 large-format books with his photos and writing, as well as in *National Geographic Magazine* and many other prestigious publications. Together, Galen and Barbara Cushman Rowell, writer and aviator, operate Mountain Light Studios in Bishop, CA. For more information about their

workshops, books and images log on to the Mountain Light website at: **www.mountainlight.com**

* * * * *

Galen and Barbara died in a tragic plane accident in August, 2002.

CARL SCOFIELD is a successful freelance photographer, in Breckenridge, CO for the past 18 years. He refers to the bulk of his work as "resort, promotional and lifestyle photography". His images have been published nationally and internationally in both books and magazines as well as advertising pieces. Carl discovered San Miguel several years ago and has returned many times to capture through photography the "culture, colors, timelessness, endurance and stoic patience of the kind, gentle people" living here. Reach Carl at: **csphoto@colorado.net**

J. BYRON SMITH is a professional location sound mixer based in Chicago. For the past 20 years, his work has taken him to six of the seven continents of the world. Though born in Texas, he just recently visited central Mexico and San Miguel, and captured not only the sounds of our town, but some images, too. For more information and to contact him directly email: **artstable@ameritech.net**

DOUGLAS STEAKLEY is a professional photographer based in Carmel Valley, CA. His images have been widely used in books, calendars, magazines, travel catalogs and postcards. Two books of his photography have recently been published: *Pacific Light* in 2000 and *Big Sur and Beyond* in 2001. Currently he is working on a new book to be titled *Mexico, Images of A Culture*. For more information about his photography please go to: **www.conceptscarmel.com**

ARTURO SUAREZ (1910-2001) captured in photos, the life and culture of San Miguel in the 1930s. He operated a photography studio for many years and taught photography at the *Instituto Allende*. For more information contact his son, Eric Suarez through: **www.smaartes.com**

LANCE TERRY grew up in Vermont and the Basque Country of Spain. He has been studying and traveling the world most of his life. Lance holds a BA in photojournalism from Arizona State University. He currently resides in San Miguel. He can be contacted at: **fotomexico_sma@hotmail.com**

WILLIAM D. THOMPSON (Memo) earned two doctorate degrees and paid his way through university in the US by working in a photographic darkroom. His love for the Mexican people, combined with his photographic and computer skills, has created an extensive digital collection of images of life here in San Miguel and the surrounding areas. In March, 2002, two of his images appeared as Kodak Picture(s) of the Day on the Kodak giant-gallery screen in Times Square. Currently, Memo is working with the local departments of tourism and rural development to develop crafts for export. To see more of Memo's work and to learn more about San Miguel and his various projects, please log on to both: **mexico.smaartes.com** and **www.labag.com**

RAUL TOUZON, a Cuban-born documentary photographer and teacher, specializes in color images. He lived in Mexico for five years and has traveled extensively documenting cultures in Latin America and the Caribbean while working for the Eastman Kodak company. Raul is an instructor for the Santa Fe Photographic Workshops and runs its Mexico operations in San Miguel. He freelances for National Geographic Magazine and has built an extensive collection of dramatic photographs which have been used in many international, corporate and editorial publications. Currently Raul lives in Florida and can be reached at: **touzonphoto@aol.com**

DON WOLF is a well-respected New Mexico photographer. Over the past twenty years, he has exhibited extensively in the US and abroad, most frequently in Santa Fe and San Miguel. His images have appeared seven times in *Photographers Forum Best of Photography Annual*. Don is primarily a street photographer whose photos reflect a keen eye for the juxtaposition of incongruous elements. He prints his own images and always uses a full frame format so he can share with the viewer exactly what he discovered in his viewfinder. You can contact Don at: **wolfstudios2002@yahoo.com**

Textile artist **SONDRA ZELL** began visiting San Miguel in the early 1990s to escape the cold, wet winters of New York City. When she retired here a few years later. Sondra continued her creative work producing monoprints, collages and mixed media pieces. Sondra finds inspiration in the quality of light, profusion of colors and the physical beauty of her new environment and community. Sondra can be reached at: **sondra@unisono.net.mx**